MY SERENDIPITY JOURNAL

by _____
(You're the author!)

with Serendipity Guide, Allyson Apsey

My Serendipity Journal
©2020 by Allyson Apsey

All rights reserved. No part of this publication may be reproduced in any form or by any electronic or mechanical means, including information storage and retrieval systems, without permission in writing by the publisher, except by a reviewer who may quote brief passages in a review. For information regarding permission, contact the publisher at info@gypsyheartpress.com.

> This book is available at special discounts when purchased in quantity for use as premiums, promotions, fundraisers, or for educational use. For inquiries and details, contact the publisher at info@gypsyheartpress.com.

Published by Gypsy Heart Press
Livingston, Texas
GypsyHeartPress.com

Cover Design by Genesis Kohler
Editing and Interior Design by Gypsy Heart Press

Library of Congress Control Number: 2019957236
Paperback ISBN: 978-1-950714-12-4

First Printing: January 2020

INTRODUCTION

The dictionary defines *serendipity* as "the occurrence of happy accidents" or "finding fortune by chance." I define serendipity a little differently. *(Side note: one of the great joys of being a writer is the creative freedom it gives you! You can even make up your own definitions for words! I can't wait to hear how you use your creative freedom in this notebook!)* I think of serendipity as a mindset, a way of thinking and living. If we look for beautiful lessons and happy accidents in everything we experience, we will live more fulfilled, happier, and wiser lives.

This journal is all yours. Use in whatever way helps you find fulfillment and happiness. The questions and quotes are there to help spark your creativity. Feel free to use them or disregard them and do your own thing. The only thing I ask is that you share some of your reflections and genius with me using #SerendipityEDU and tagging me @AllysonApsey.

I am better because of you! Now, it's time to release *your* creative serendipity. Enjoy every minute.

♥ Allyson Apsey

My Serendipity Journal

What is the most awkward or quirky thing about you? How do you laugh yourself through embarrassment?

Date: _____

Picture of my
awkward self

My Serendipity Journal

"That which does not kill us, makes us stronger."
—Friedrich Nietzsche

Date: _____

> "Don't be afraid of your imperfect humanness. It is a gift."
> —Allyson Apsey, *Through the Lens of Serendipity*

My Serendipity Journal

What is your favorite way to relax?

Date: _____

My favorite
way to chill

My Serendipity Journal

Date: _____

"Your success and happiness lies in you. Resolve to keep happy, and your joy and you shall form an invincible host against difficulties."
—Helen Keller

My Serendipity Journal

What is the most daring thing you have ever done? What did it teach you about yourself?

Date: _____

My Serendipity Journal

> "I've found that luck is quite predictable. If you want more luck, take more chances. Be more active. Show up more often."
> —Brian Tracy

Date: _____

This is me being daring ↘

"What people call serendipity sometimes is just having your eyes open."
—José Manuel Barroso

My Serendipity Journal

Where have you found serendipity in your own life? (Serendipity is the phenomenon of finding "happy accidents," and it is often found when something that first appears to be negative actually ends up being positive.)

Date: _____

My Serendipity Journal

"Live everyday like it's Taco Tuesday."
—Unknown

Date: _____

My favorite food ↳→

My Serendipity Journal

What is your favorite song?
What emotions does it evoke?

Date: _____

My Serendipity Journal

"When the sharpest words wanna cut me down, I'm gonna send a flood, gonna drown them out..."
—Keala Settle and *The Greatest Showman* Ensemble

Date: _____

My Serendipity Journal

What is the best thing about your family?

Date: _____

My Family

My Serendipity Journal

> "It is really hard to not allow others' behavior to invade your thoughts and feelings. But I am strong enough to make my internal voice of hope and love and gratitude louder than their voices."
> —Kip, from *The Serendipity Journal* by Allyson Apsey

Date: _____

"Should you ever look up and find yourself lost, simply take a breath and start over. Retrace your steps and go back to the purest place in your heart where your hope lives. You will find your way again."
—Unknown

My Serendipity Journal

How could you tell your family what you love about them?

Date: _____

My Serendipity Journal

"Laughter is the closest distance between two people."
—Victor Borge

Date: _____

My favorite
person to
laugh with
↪

My Serendipity Journal

Which family members or friends feel like sunshine to be around?
How could you surround yourself with people like that more often?

Date: _____

My Serendipity Journal

"Nothing is so bad that we cannot face it with gratitude and dignity, keeping the needs of others at the forefront of all we do."
—Allyson Apsey, *The Path to Serendipity*

Date: _____

My Serendipity Journal

Have you ever experienced something so hurtful that you weren't sure how to respond or what to do? How did you handle the situation?

Date: _____

My Serendipity Journal

"When they go low,
we go high."
—Michelle Obama

Date: _____

Me, feeling strong →

"I am going to choose every day to love myself. I am imperfect, just like you, but I am determined to improve every day and to work hard not to take my own struggles out on the people around me."
—Kip, from *The Serendipity Journal* by Allyson Apsey

My Serendipity Journal

Name the trusted people you feel comfortable turning to when you aren't sure how to handle a situation. What characteristics do they have that helps you trust them?

Date: _____

My Serendipity Journal

"What the world needs most is openness: Open hearts, open doors, open eyes, open minds, open ears, open souls."
—Robert Muller

Date: _____

My Serendipity Journal

Think of a situation you have experienced that felt out of control. How did you gain back control over that situation?

Date:_____

My Serendipity Journal

"When you feel sad, it's okay. It's not the end of the world. Everyone has those days when you doubt yourself, and when you feel like everything you do sucks, but then there's those days when you feel like Superman. It's just the balance of the world. I just write to feel better."
—Mac Miller

Date: _____

My Serendipity Journal

Date: _____

> "Any fool can criticize, condemn and complain—and most fools do."
> —Benjamin Franklin

My Serendipity Journal

When has a great challenge in your life worked out to a happy ending?
What do you think you did to help create that positive outcome?

Date: _____

"People who do cruel things do not feel good about themselves."
—Kip, from *The Serendipity Journal* by Allyson Apsey

My Serendipity Journal

"The words we tell ourselves have even more power than the words we tell others."
—Allyson Apsey, *Through the Lens of Serendipity*

Date: _____

People who feel like sunshine

"Hold the door, say please, say thank you
Don't steal, don't cheat, and don't lie;
I know you got mountains to climb, but
Always stay humble and kind."
—Tim McGraw

My Serendipity Journal

What goal are you ready to crush?
What is your first step?

Date: _____

My Serendipity Journal

Date: _____

Me, crushing my goals ⟶

"All you need to do is move inch by inch toward the person you want to become. That is enough. YOU are enough."
—Allyson Apsey, *The Path to Serendipity*